Amazing Planet Earth

MASSIVE MOUNTAINS

TERRY JENNINGS

W

FRANKLIN WATTS

LONDON • SYDNEY

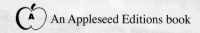 An Appleseed Editions book

First published in 2009 by Franklin Watts

Franklin Watts
338 Euston Road, London NW1 3BH

Franklin Watts Australia
Level 17/207 Kent St, Sydney, NSW 2000

© 2009 Appleseed Editions

Appleseed Editions Ltd
Well House, Friars Hill, Guestling, East Sussex TN35 4ET

Created by Q2AMedia
Book Editor: Michael Downey
Art Director: Rahul Dhiman
Designers: Ritu Chopra, Ranjan Singh
Picture Researcher: Shreya Sharma
Line Artist: Sibi N. Devasia
Colouring Artist: Mahender Kumar

ISBN 978 0 7496 8808 0

Dewey classification: 551.43'2

All words in **bold** can be found in Glossary on pages 30–31.

Website information is correct at time of going to press. However, the publishers cannot
accept liability for any information or links found on third-party websites.

A CIP catalogue for this book is available from the British Library.

Picture credits
t=top b=bottom c=centre l=left r=right
Cover Image: Alessio Ponti/ Shutterstock.
Back Cover: shutterstock

Insides: Nathan Jaskowiak/ Shutterstock: Title Page, Nathan Jaskowiak/ Shutterstock: 4-5, Jorg Jahn/ Shutterstock: 6, Associated Press:
7t, Steffen Foerster Photography/ Shutterstock: 8, National Geographic/ Getty Images: 9, iStockphoto: 12, Earth Observatory/ NASA:
13, Ilya D. Gridnev/ Shutterstock: 15b, Cristina/ Shutterstock: 16, Wolfgang Amri/ Shutterstock: 17, Michael Shake/ Shutterstock: 18,
Karen Kasmauski/ Corbis: 19, Amygdala Imagery/ Shutterstock: 20, Urosr/ Shutterstock: 21, Dwi Oblo / Reuters: 22, Associated Press:
23, David P. Lewis/ Shutterstock: 25, Corbis Sygma: 26, Bmflv Minich/ Associated Press: 27, Steve Estvanik/ 123rf: 28,
Jorg Jahn/ Shutterstock: 31.
Q2AMedia Art Bank: 7b, 10, 11, 14, 15t, 24.

Printed in China

Franklin Watts is a division of Hachette Children's Books,
an Hachette UK company.
www.hachette.co.uk

Contents

Beauty and danger

Mountains are some of the most beautiful places on the Earth. But they can also be extremely dangerous. Freezing temperatures and high winds can be deadly for even the most experienced climbers.

Magic mountains

Mountains make up a quarter of the Earth's surface. There are even mountain **ranges** under the world's oceans. All of the world's largest rivers begin life in the mountains, and mountains have a big effect on the weather. Forestry companies grow trees on mountain slopes and get wood from them. Mining companies dig out valuable minerals from mountains.

• The Andes are the world's longest mountain chain. They stretch for 8,900 km along the western side of South America.

Life and death

As soon as a mountain is formed, it begins to wear away. Little by little, the mountain crumbles away. The pieces are carried down by the wind, rivers and **glaciers**, eventually finishing up in oceans. These changes in mountains usually take place very slowly. But sometimes, mountains change with terrifying speed, putting in danger the lives of people who live and work near them.

DATA FILE

- Mountains occur in 75 per cent of the world's countries.

- Mountains are made of solid **rock**. Hills can be made of solid rock or from rock fragments built up by glaciers or by wind.

- More than half of all fresh water comes from mountains.

- One in ten of the world's population live near mountains.

- Mountain **peaks** are always very cold and often covered in snow.

The Himalayas

Name: The Himalayas
Location: Asia
Length: 2,500 km
Age: 30–50 million years old
Mountain type: Fold
Highest mountain: Mount Everest, 8,848 m

The Himalayas contain many of the world's highest peaks. The tallest is Mount Everest. These mountains form a gigantic barrier of rock that separates India and Nepal from Tibet.

Giant humps

Millions of years ago, the Himalayas were not mountains. They were flat areas of land at the bottom of a shallow ocean. The Himalayas started to grow about 50 million years ago when two sections of the Earth's **crust** started crunching against each other. This forced up the layers of rock to form giant humps and folds that we now know as the Himalayas.

• Mount Everest lies among the snow-covered peaks of the Himalayas.

• In 1953, New Zealander Edmund Hillary and Tenzing Norgay from Nepal were the first people to reach the top of Everest.

Monsoon rains

For four months each year, monsoon winds blow north over the Himalayas. These cause heavy rain and snow to fall on the southern side of the Himalayas. That is why there are lush tropical forests and snow-covered peaks on the southern side. By the time the winds reach the northern side of the Himalayas, they have lost most of their moisture. On these north-facing slopes, there is dry desert.

• Monsoon winds release most of their rain on the southern slopes of the Himalayas.

Heavy rain

Dry winds

Parched desert

Wet winds

Not enough wood

Several big rivers are fed by the ice and snow that covers much of the Himalayas. Hundreds of millions of people in India, Pakistan and Bangladesh get their water from these rivers. But the Himalayas are changing. In the last 30 to 40 years, the population of Nepal, on the southern slopes of the Himalayas, has doubled. There is now not enough food and firewood to go around. More than two-thirds of the trees have been cut down for firewood and to make new fields.

Overflowing rivers

Normally, tree roots soak up water and hold soil in place. Now, with many fewer trees in the Himalayas, soil is washed into the rivers when it rains. This makes the rivers overflow, causing flooding in the **valleys** and plains across India and Bangladesh. In Nepal, entire villages have been swept away by torrents from overflowing rivers.

● In Nepal, the lower slopes of the Himalayas have been cut into steps to stop soil from being washed away by overflowing rivers.

Litter problem

A big problem on Mount Everest and other Himalayan mountains is the litter that is left by the many climbing expeditions and tourists that visit the area. Over the years, a huge quantity of litter has collected. Because it is so cold, the litter does not rot or rust away.

• Many gas and oxygen canisters have been dumped by mountain climbers on Mount Everest.

• According to one expedition leader, there are at least 200 tonnes of litter on the higher slopes of Everest, making it the world's highest rubbish dump.

• Mountaineers have left behind more than 50,000 glass bottles, ropes, tents, food packaging and even a wrecked helicopter.

• In 1998, the Nepalese government imposed a ban on taking bottled drinks to the Mount Everest region.

Fold and block mountains

The Earth's crust is made up of huge slabs of rock called plates. These move very slowly, sometimes crashing into each other, sometimes moving apart. It is the movement of these plates that has caused all mountains to form.

Fold mountains

The Earth's **plates** float on the very hot rocks below them and make very small movements each year. When two of these plates crash, the layers of rock may be pushed up and folded over each other, like a giant rumpled blanket. This folding can make several long rows of mountains, called **fold mountains**. The highest mountains are in the middle, with smaller mountains on either side and rows of hills beyond. The Himalayas, the European Alps and the Appalachians in the USA are all fold mountains.

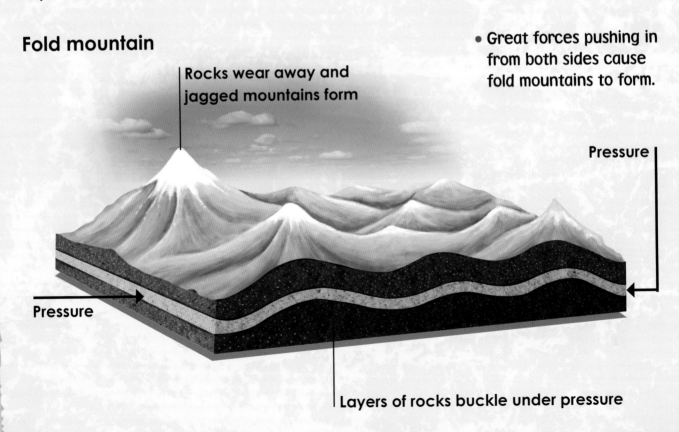

Fold mountain

Rocks wear away and jagged mountains form

• Great forces pushing in from both sides cause fold mountains to form.

Pressure

Pressure

Layers of rocks buckle under pressure

Block mountains

As the Earth's plates push and pull against each other, rocks sometimes crack under the strain. These cracks are called faults. When two faults are close together, the chunk of the Earth's crust between them can sometimes collapse to form a rift valley. Or, if the plates shove together, they may squeeze a great slab of rock up. The raised parts are called **block mountains**. The Sierra Nevada mountains in the USA and the Harz mountains in Germany are block mountains. They were formed long ago during what must have been some of the world's biggest ever earthquakes.

Block mountain

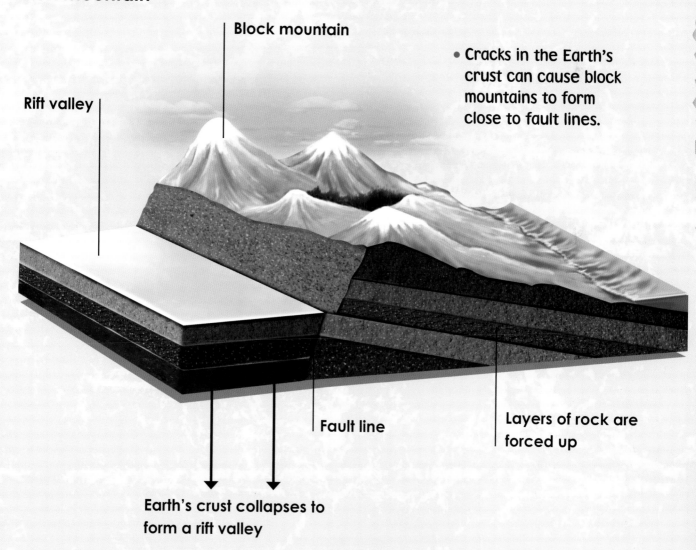

Block mountain

Rift valley

• Cracks in the Earth's crust can cause block mountains to form close to fault lines.

Fault line

Layers of rock are forced up

Earth's crust collapses to form a rift valley

Mount Kilimanjaro

Mount Kilimanjaro is a record-breaker. At 5,895 metres high, this extinct volcano is the world's highest free-standing mountain. It is also the tallest mountain in Africa.

Steam and sulphur dioxide

Mount Kilimanjaro is the largest **volcano** in a belt of about 20 volcanoes in East Africa. Kilimanjaro formed between about 1.8 million and 10,000 years ago. Although Mount Kilimanjaro is an extinct volcano, steam and **sulphur dioxide** still stream from it. Even though the mountain is very near to the Equator, until recently its summit always had a covering of snow and ice.

• Snow covers the top of Tanzania's Mount Kilimanjaro for a short time each year.

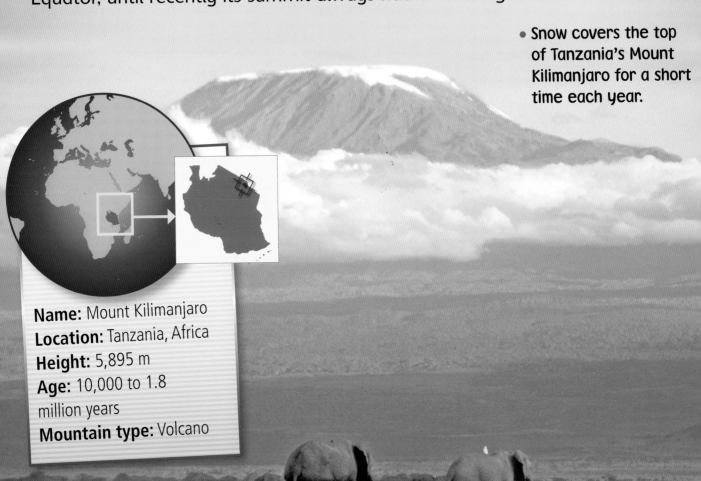

Name: Mount Kilimanjaro
Location: Tanzania, Africa
Height: 5,895 m
Age: 10,000 to 1.8 million years
Mountain type: Volcano

Disappearing ice

During the 20th century, Mount Kilimanjaro's ice cap shrunk dramatically. In 1912, the ice covered a huge area measuring more than 10 square kilometres. Since then, four-fifths of the ice cap has disappeared, leaving just small patches. At this rate, scientists think that the ice at the top of Kilimanjaro will be completely gone by 2020. Then there will not be enough **meltwater** to keep rivers and springs running all year round.

- The ice-cap on the summit of Mount Kilimanjaro is shrinking fast.

News Flash

Sky News, 15 March 2005

The snow-capped summit of Mount Kilimanjaro has melted away to reveal the tip of the African peak for the first time in 11,000 years. The glaciers and snow, which kept the summit white, have almost completely disappeared. Although scientists had predicted the melt would happen, it is 15 years sooner than they had predicted. The white peak of the 5,895 metres mountain has long formed a stunning part of Tanzanian landscape.

Volcanic and dome mountains

Below the Earth's crust is a layer of rock called the mantle. Parts of the mantle are so hot that the rock has melted to form a gooey substance called magma. When magma comes up to the surface, it can form spectacular mountains.

Volcanic mountain

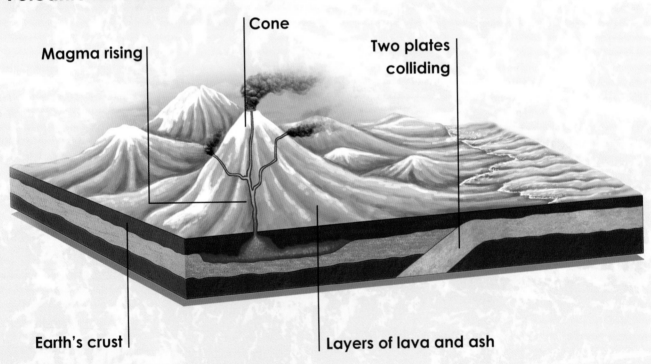

Cone

Magma rising

Two plates colliding

Earth's crust

Layers of lava and ash

Volcanic mountains

A volcanic mountain forms when molten rock, or **magma**, from deep inside the Earth escapes to the surface. When it reaches the surface, the magma is called lava. Most volcanoes are found at weak points in the Earth's crust, where two or more plates crash together or move apart. Like Mount Kilimanjaro, Mount St. Helens in the USA and Mount Pinatubo in the Philippines were also formed by volcanoes.

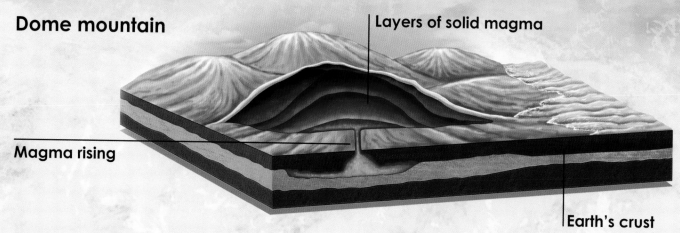

Dome mountain

Layers of solid magma

Magma rising

Earth's crust

Dome mountains

If a huge amount of magma pushes its way upwards, it may collect just beneath the Earth's surface like a gigantic blister. This magma cools into solid rock and forms a **dome mountain**. Unlike a volcano, the magma under a dome mountain does not have enough force to make it to the surface. Navajo Mountain in the USA and Showashinzan in Japan are examples of dome mountains.

- Showashinzan in Japan is a dome mountain. It is like a gigantic blister filled with solid magma.

DATA FILE

- The Earth's surface is made up of seven major plates and many minor plates.

- Plates move from a few millimetres to about 13 cm a year.

- A plate moving at 5 cm a year will travel 50 km in a million years.

- Some large mountain ranges, such as the Andes in South America and the Rocky Mountains in the USA, lie close to the edges of major plates.

European Alps

The Alps are the largest mountain chain in Europe. They stretch for 1,000 kilometres from Austria and Slovenia in the east to Germany and France in the west.

Huge valleys and lakes

The European Alps, which formed between 33 and 15 million years ago, have several peaks more than 4,000 metres high. At 4,807 metres, Mont Blanc in France is the highest peak. Over the last two million years, the mountain landscape has been changed by glaciers. Working like gigantic bulldozers, these rivers of ice have carved out deep U-shaped valleys and huge lakes, such as Lake Como and Lake Garda.

Name: European Alps
Location: South-central Europe
Length: 1,000 km
Age: 15–33 million years
Mountain type: Fold
Highest mountain: Mont Blanc, France, 4,807 m

• About 20,000 mountaineers climb France's Mont Blanc every year.

Skiing, hiking and biking

The Alps are very popular for sightseeing and sports. During the winter, you can see people skiing, snowboarding, tobogganing and snowshoeing. In summer, the Alps are popular with hikers, mountain bikers, paragliders and mountaineers. Many of the lakes attract swimmers, sailors and windsurfers. The lower areas and larger towns of the Alps are easy to reach by motorways and roads. To make it easier to get about, tunnels have been cut through the Alps to allow travel at all times of the year.

• From December to April, skiing is a popular sport in the European Alps.

DATA FILE

- Many of Europe's large rivers, including the Rhine and the Danube, start in the Alps.

- Alpine waterfalls and rivers are used to generated electricity.

- Below the snowline are pastures used for grazing cattle and sheep in summer.

- In Alpine valleys and foothills, crops are planted. Grapes are grown on some sunny slopes.

- In 1991, the body of a man was found in ice in the Alps. A bow, arrows and a copper axe were nearby. Scientists later discovered the man had died 5,200 years ago!

Appalachian Mountains

The Appalachians are a great mountain range that runs along the east coast of North America, from the province of Quebec in Canada to Alabama in southern USA.

Name: Appalachian Mountains
Location: Atlantic coast of North America
Length: 2,400 km
Age: 300 million years
Mountain type: Fold
Highest mountain: Mount Mitchell, North Carolina, 2,037 m

Forest and farmland

As mountains go, the Appalachians are quite tame. They are low and gentle with an average height of only 900 metres. They are special, however, because they cover a huge area, about 2,400 kilometres long and sometimes more than 400 kilometres wide. Much of the range is covered by dense forest. The Great Appalachian Valley, which runs the length of the mountains, contains extremely fertile farmland. The Appalachians are very popular with hikers. The Appalachian Trail, which runs for 3,500 kilometres from Maine to Georgia, takes up to six months to complete!

• Much of the Appalachian Mountain range is covered in thick forest.

Rocks and minerals

Not all parts of the Appalachians are beautiful, however. The mountains contain huge deposits of valuable rocks and minerals, including iron ore, coal, slate, limestone, oil and gas. To get coal, about 470 mountains have been blown up and levelled in recent years. Before the coal can be mined, the forest is first bulldozed. The topsoil is then scraped away and explosives are set off in the rocks below. The rubble is then tipped into the valleys. More than 7,000 valleys have already been filled and some 1,100 kilometres of rivers and streams have disappeared under rubble or have been polluted with toxic waste.

DATA FILE

- The Appalachians are one of the oldest mountain chains on Earth.

- The name Appalachian comes from the Apalachee tribe, who were the first inhabitants of the area.

- The Appalachian Mountain range does not have any volcanoes.

- Many Appalachian streams are used to make hydroelectric power.

- Farms and orchards are found in the valley bottoms. Potatoes and wheat are grown in the north. In the south, farmers grow maize and tobacco and raise poultry.

● In the Appalachians, miners have sliced off the tops of mountains to reach mineral deposits.

Weathering and erosion

Mountains may seem solid and permanent, but they begin to crumble almost as soon as they rise. Weaknesses appear in the rocks, which let in air and water. This starts a process called weathering.

Breaking rocks

When water gets into small cracks in rocks, it makes these wider. This is because when water freezes, it expands as it turns into ice. Eventually, pieces of rock break off and slide down a mountain's steep slopes. This loose rock is called **scree**. Wind, rivers and glaciers carry a lot of the rock fragments away from the mountains. Most of it finishes up at the bottom of the sea.

● At 4,418 m, craggy Mount Whitney is the highest mountain in the Sierra Nevada range in the USA.

Jagged to rounded

As pieces of rock break away from mountains, jagged peaks are left. Over time, however, even these jagged peaks are worn away to leave softly rounded mountain tops. The Himalayas, the Andes and the European Alps still have jagged peaks that have not been eroded very much. The Appalachians in the USA and Australia's Uluru, or Ayers Rock, on the other hand, have been worn down over millions of years.

- Uluru, or Ayers Rock, in Australia is only 348 m high. It was formed 300 million years ago and was once much higher, but has slowly worn away.

DATA FILE

- No movement is involved in **weathering**, but as soon as the loosened rock material starts to move due to wind, moving water or ice, it is called **erosion**.

- The world's rivers carry about 20 billion tonnes of loose rock fragments, or sediment, to the oceans each year.

- All mountains slowly erode. One result of this is that they gradually lose weight. When this happens, the Earth's crust slowly pushes the mountain upwards.

Landslides in Java

Landslides are common in Indonesia. But in December 2007, days of torrential monsoon rains and flooding caused the most devastating landslides in the area for 25 years.

Name: Java landslides
Location: Java, Indonesia
Type of disaster: Landslide
Deadly event: December 2007
Fatalities: At least 120

Java at risk

Landslides often happen in Indonesia during the rainy season. As rain batters the sides of a mountain, it soaks the ground. This causes huge chunks of earth to break away. The inhabitants of the island of Java are always at risk because so many people live on the lower slopes of mountains and in the valleys. The removal of the trees from muddy mountain slopes has made the problem worse.

● Rescuers search for survivors in the mud left by the Java landslides.

Deadly mud

In December 2007, many days of torrential rain caused severe flooding and landslides across Java. The flooding was made worse by extra high ocean tides. Tens of thousands of people were left homeless. They had to wade through chest-high water, clutching their belongings above their heads. The worst single incident was in the Karanganyar district, where 67 people were killed in a landslide on a mountain slope. The victims were buried in mud up to 5 metres deep. Local people had to use their hands and simple tools to rescue those trapped. In Java as a whole, at least 120 people died in the landslides.

News Flash

ABC (Australian Broadcasting Company) News
Thursday, 27 December 2007

Rescue teams in Indonesia are trying to reach dozens of people buried in landslides on the island of Java after floods and landslides left nearly 100 people dead or missing. Officials say landslides hit villages in densely populated central Java's Karanganyar and Wonogiri districts early on Wednesday.

• Mud and rocks dumped by the Java landslides buried this house nearly to its roof.

What causes landslides?

Weathered pieces of rock slide down a mountain when they break off. Usually the pieces collect in one place until rains, melting snow or an earthquake start them moving downwards. Sometimes, this happens at great speed.

Rock falls

We have already seen how pieces of rock, or scree, break away from the mountain and collect at the foot of the slope. After many years they form a cone-shaped pile, called a scree slope. There are many small **rock falls** on the slopes of a mountain. They are most common in the spring when ice that has formed in cracks in the rocks begins to melt, releasing the pieces of rock. They also occur after heavy rain has soaked the soil or rock, making it heavier.

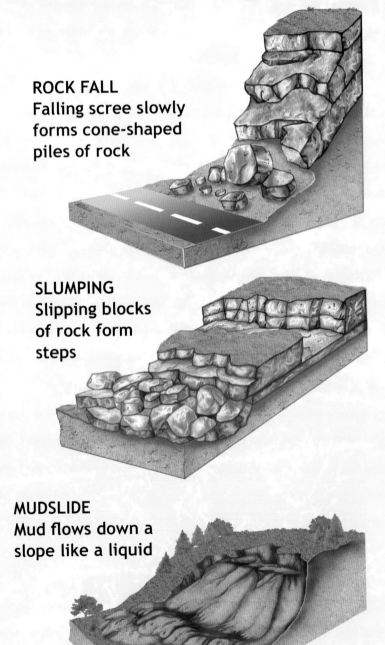

ROCK FALL
Falling scree slowly forms cone-shaped piles of rock

SLUMPING
Slipping blocks of rock form steps

MUDSLIDE
Mud flows down a slope like a liquid

- These three kinds of landslide show how rocks and soil can move down a slope.

Slumping

When a huge block of rock falls during a landslide, it is called slumping. Often set off by an earthquake, slumping is most common where a layer of rock, with lots of cracks and joints in it, lies on top of a layer of smoother, slippery rock such as clay or **shale**. The slumping blocks of rock may be up to 3 kilometres long and 150 metres thick. Such a slump often leaves large steps down the side of a mountain.

Mudslides

Mudslides usually happen after a heavy rainstorm or when snow melts rapidly on a mountain. The soil or other loose material then becomes soaked with water. Some mudslides are caused by water mixing with the ash from a volcano. The wet material no longer sticks to the slope and slides downwards, flowing like a liquid.

DATA FILE

- The digging of mines and quarries in mountains, or forest clearing from mountain slopes, can start a landslide. They can also make one worse than it would have been.

- Mudslides, which are pulled down by the force of gravity, can travel at speeds greater than 75 km/h.

- A series of landslides in 1920 in China killed 100,000 people and destroyed many villages.

- Rock falls are most likely to happen when ice melts higher up a mountain, allowing weakened rocks to fall.

Deadly avalanche

In 1999, a huge avalanche struck the small town of Galtür in the Austrian Alps. Galtür was buried under 5 metres of snow and 31 people were killed.

Hidden block of snow

January 1999 was a warm month in the Austrian Alps. But this was followed by record snowfalls and strong winds in February. The unlucky people of Galtür did not know that a huge and unstable block of snow was forming high up on one of the mountain slopes above the town.

- The inhabitants of Galtür had little warning of the devastating snow avalanche.

Name: Galtür avalanche
Location: Galtür, Austria
Type of disaster: Avalanche
Deadly event: February 1999
Fatalities: 31

Lucky survivors

On 23 February, rising temperatures and showers of rain loosened the block of snow. The block, which scientists believe weighed about 170,000 tonnes, began to move down the slope. It picked up speed until it reached nearly 300 km/h. It took less than a minute to hit the valley below, by which time it had doubled in size. This **avalanche** buried Galtür under 5 metres of snow. Houses and other buildings were crushed, roads were blocked and telephone lines were brought down. For a whole night, rescue helicopters could not reach the disaster zone because of raging snowstorms. Amazingly, 26 victims were dug out alive.

News Flash

BBC News, 24 February 1999

At least eight people have been killed after twin avalanches hit the small town of Galtür in the Alps in western Austria. It is thought that more than 25 others are still trapped under snow, but even before night fell, the rescue operation was being hampered by bad weather and fading light.

● A specially trained dog searches for avalanche victims. It takes a dog half an hour to search an area that it would take 20 people four hours to cover.

What causes avalanches?

An avalanche is a mass of ice or snow that suddenly crashes down the side of a mountain into the valley below. Many avalanches sweep along chunks of rock, which makes them even more dangerous.

Powder avalanche

There are two main kinds of snow and ice avalanche. The first kind is known as a **powder avalanche**. This type of avalanche can happen in very cold, dry weather when light powdery grains of snow do not stick together. If this snow starts to move down the mountain, it forms a powdery mass of snow that swirls along like an enormous white cloud.

• A huge powder avalanche on Alaska's Mount McKinley.

Slab avalanche

The second kind of avalanche is called a **slab avalanche**. This starts as a solid chunk of frozen snow about the size of a **soccer pitch** and about 9 metres thick. It often forms when sunny days are followed by frosty nights. This change in temperature causes melted snow to freeze again. When this massive slab suddenly starts sliding down a mountain at great speed, it often carries huge rocks and trees with it.

Avalanche wind

When an avalanche is rushing down a mountain, a big wind is produced ahead of the mass of snow or ice. This is known as an avalanche wind. This wind is often strong enough to demolish entire buildings.

DATA FILE

- The average speed of an avalanche is 100 km/h. But the maximum recorded speed is 392 km/h.

- There are up to one million avalanches worldwide each year and they kill about 100 people.

- To help prevent avalanches, fences made of wood, aluminium or steel are built on steep slopes where snow collects in deep drifts.

- Guns or small explosives are sometimes used to set off safe, harmless avalanches.

- Forests of large, mature trees growing on mountain slopes form one of the best protections against avalanches.

- A destructive avalanche wind will rush down a mountain ahead of an avalanche such as this.

Glossary

avalanche a sudden fall of snow down the side of a mountain

block mountains mountains that have been formed where land has been pushed up close to a fault, or between two faults

crust the outer layer of the Earth, made up of huge slabs of rock

dome mountain a shallow, rounded mountain formed from a huge quantity of liquid rock that is pushed up under the Earth's crust

erosion the natural wearing away of land by wind, moving water or ice. The eroded material is carried away and dropped in other places

fold mountains mountains that have been thrown up into huge folds, or ridges, by movements of the Earth's plates

glacier a large river of slow-moving ice, or ice and rock, that forms in a mountain and moves very slowly down a valley

landslide soil or rocks sliding down the side of a hill or mountain

magma the hot, molten rock formed in the Earth's mantle, just below the crust

meltwater water that is released from melting snow and ice

oxygen colourless, odourless and tasteless gas that is essential for the survival of almost all living creatures

peak the pointed top of a mountain

plates the sections of the Earth's crust that fit together like the pieces of a giant jigsaw puzzle

powder avalanche an avalanche made up of powdery grains of snow that do not stick together

range a row, or line, of mountains

rock the solid part of the Earth's crust beneath the soil

rock fall fragments of rock, or scree, that break away from the face of a steep cliff, hill or mountain and collect at the foot of the slope

scree pieces of weathered rock that collect at the bottom of a steep mountain slope

shale a soft rock made of solid mud

slab avalanche an avalanche that consists of a huge slab of frozen snow

soccer pitch this is about 120 metres by 90 metres

summit the top of a mountain or hill

sulphur dioxide a smelly gas that is released from volcanoes, especially during eruptions

valley a low-lying strip of land between steep hills or mountains. A river, stream or glacier may run along the bottom

volcano a hole or tear in the Earth's crust from which molten rock flows

weathering the breaking up of rocks by heat, cold, ice and rainwater

31

Index

Webfinder

www.rocksforkids.com/RFK/TableofContents.html
A good starting point for learning about rocks and minerals

www.mountain.org/education/explore.htm
Discover the secrets of mountains, including their folklore

www.fema.gov/hazard/
All about disasters and how to protect yourself against them

http://education.usgs.gov/common/primary.htm
A website covering a wide range of subjects, including landslides